KIDDYWINK CREW

ALPHABET & NUMBER PRACTICE

I0171577

Dear Caretaker,

So glad you purchased this practice packet! Your child will surely benefit from the letter and number recognition practice.

There are extension opportunities throughout:
-Talk about the letter *sounds*.
-Come up with words that start with each letter.
-Have them practice writing letters outside of the packet without tracing.
-Count out each number with a small item in your house (cheerios always work well)!

Thanks again for supporting our small business!

SCAN THE QR CODE
TO LISTEN TO
THE PODCAST!

With heart,
Julianna and Lindsay

KIDDYWINK CREW

ALPHABET & NUMBER PRACTICE

POP the correct bubbles for each page!

Example for the "A" page:

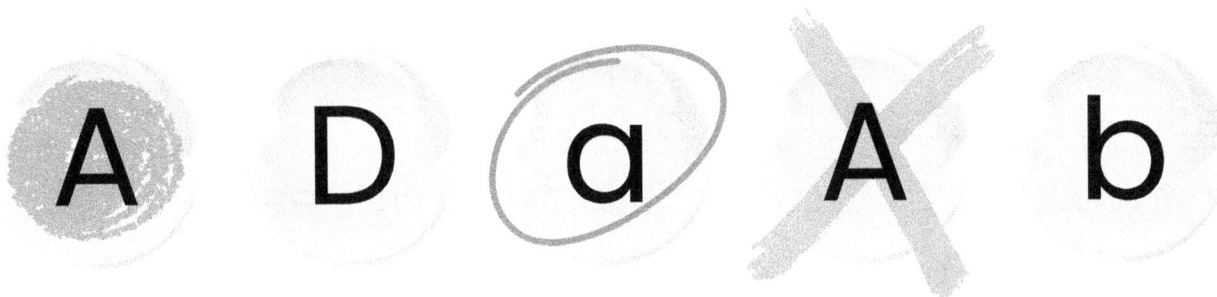

A D a A b

You can POP them using dot markers, coloring them in, circling them, or drawing an X through them. It's your choice!

Enjoy!

SCAN THE QR CODE TO LISTEN TO THE PODCAST!

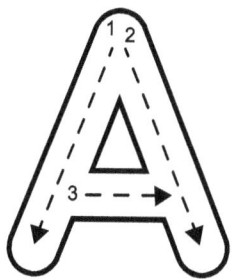

POP THE BUBBLES!

POP ALL THE BUBBLES WITH THE LETTER A!

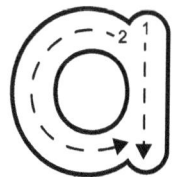

A   G   a   P   L

A   d   A   C   V

a   R   h   a   A

A   V   A   R   a

AWESOME WORK!

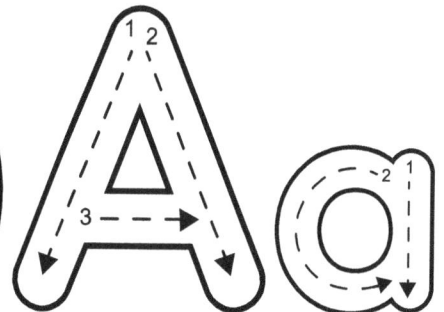

KIDDYWINK
CREW

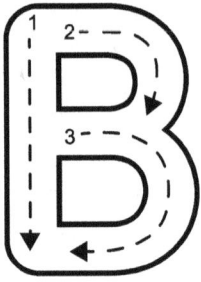

POP THE BUBBLES!

POP ALL THE BUBBLES WITH THE LETTER B!

b	B	k	d	b
B	e	S	b	B
n	B	b	B	P
B	f	B	O	b

BEAUTIFUL!

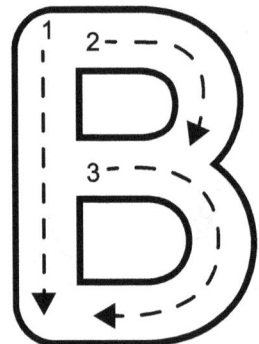

KIDDYWINK CREW

2

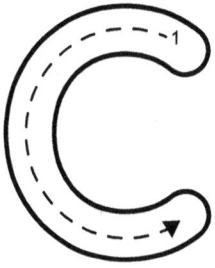

POP THE BUBBLES!

POP ALL THE BUBBLES WITH THE LETTER C!

W   B   C   O   C

D   C   S   C   i

F   C   U   c   E

c   C   G   C   j

COOL WORK!

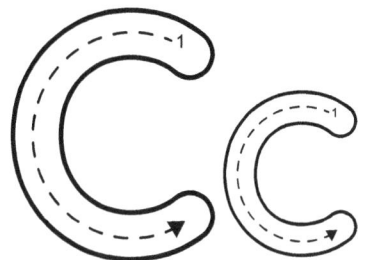

3

KIDDYWINK CREW

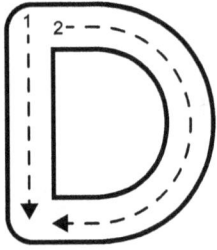

POP THE BUBBLES!

POP ALL THE BUBBLES WITH THE LETTER D!

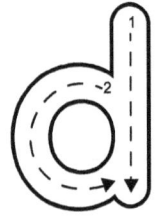

d B C Q D

D C d C y

L D d n d

c d G D j

DELIGHTFUL!

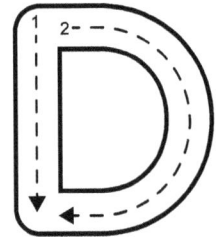
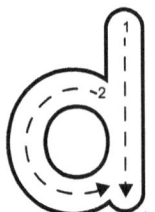

KIDDYWINK CREW

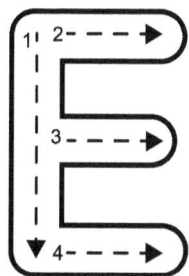

POP THE BUBBLES!

POP ALL THE BUBBLES WITH THE LETTER E!

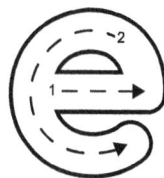

R   T   e   p   E

E   I   K   j   e

Z   e   G   h   E

e   e   G   l   i

EXCELLENT!

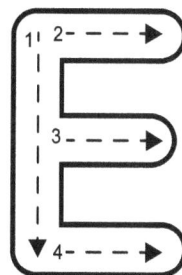

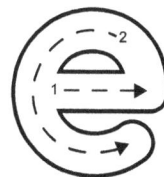

5

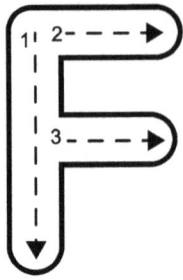

POP THE BUBBLES!

POP ALL THE BUBBLES WITH THE LETTER F!

F	B	d	f	f
w	u	i	F	c
F	f	p	L	m
M	t	f	F	j

FANTASTIC!

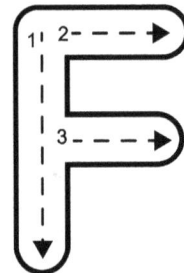

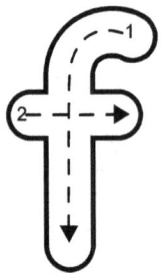

6

KIDDYWINK CREW

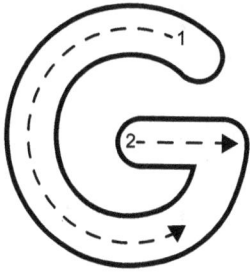

POP THE BUBBLES!

POP ALL THE BUBBLES WITH THE LETTER G!

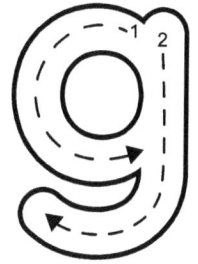

H	G	g	p	J
q	g	R	b	j
G	G	u	n	g
x	m	g	w	y

GOOD JOB!

7

KIDDYWINK CREW

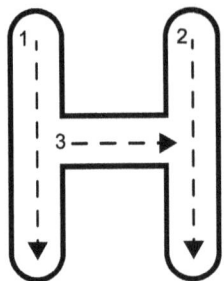

POP THE BUBBLES!

POP ALL THE BUBBLES WITH THE LETTER H!

H   p   w   h   h

b   s   k   H   l

H   h   N   f   x

n   H   h   p   e

HARD-WORKER!

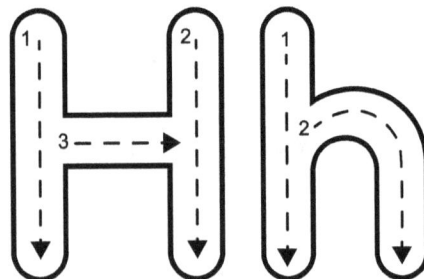

8

KIDDYWINK CREW

POP THE BUBBLES!

POP ALL THE BUBBLES WITH THE LETTER l!

k   F   l   i   P

q   l   S   c   i

i   D   a   l   w

i   J   j   t   l

IMPRESSIVE!

KIDDYWINK CREW

POP THE BUBBLES!

POP ALL THE BUBBLES WITH THE LETTER J!

J	i	A	t	j
V	b	P	j	q
J	J	b	f	j
O	Y	R	J	j

JAW-DROPPING!

10

KIDDYWINK CREW

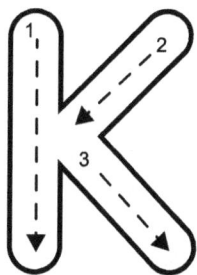

POP THE BUBBLES!

POP ALL THE BUBBLES WITH THE LETTER K!

K   l   P   k   q

W   E   K   J   K

k   v   n   b   K

x   K   z   K   F

KUDOS!

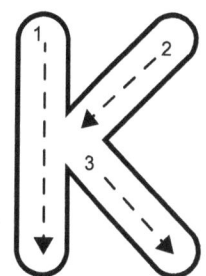

11

KIDDYWINK CREW

POP THE BUBBLES!

POP ALL THE BUBBLES WITH THE LETTER L!

k L r n L

d l q n L

L u y l v

l L t T c

LOVELY!

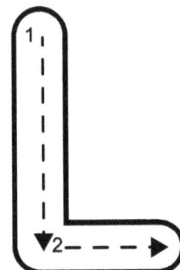

12

KIDDYWINK CREW

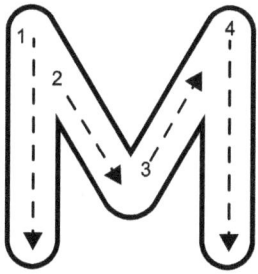

POP THE BUBBLES!

POP ALL THE BUBBLES WITH THE LETTER m!

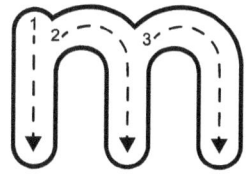

r M n M m

o p w M v

m e m N x

m M Y b j

MAGNIFICENT!

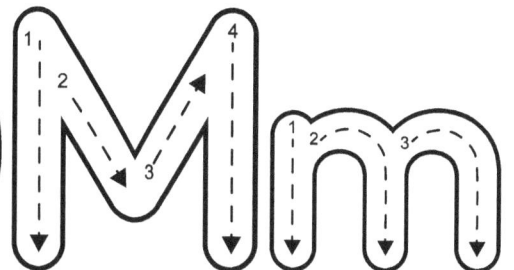

13

KIDDYWINK
CREW

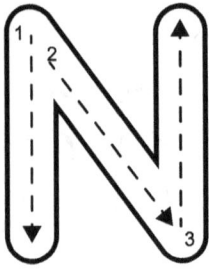

POP THE BUBBLES!

POP ALL THE BUBBLES WITH THE LETTER N!

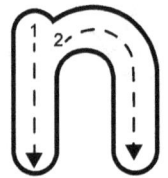

M	J	K	n	N
f	v	b	N	n
u	n	N	r	b
C	Y	n	N	W

NICE JOB!

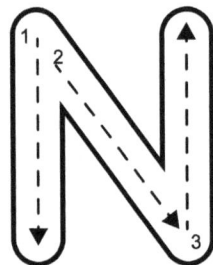

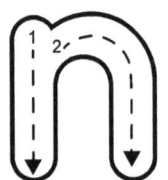

14

KIDDYWINK CREW

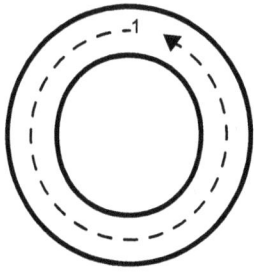

POP THE BUBBLES!

POP ALL THE BUBBLES WITH THE LETTER O!

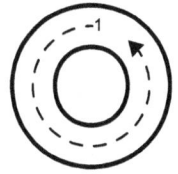

O T Q O C

D O o q b

O f G h o

p E o O j

OKAY!

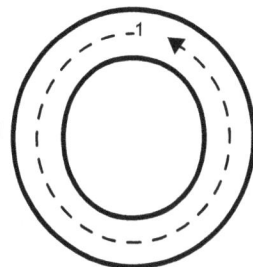

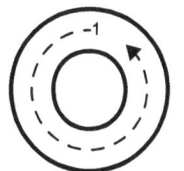

15

KIDDYWINK
CREW

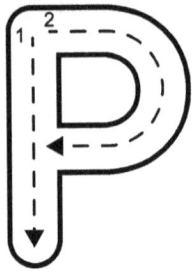

POP THE BUBBLES!

POP ALL THE BUBBLES WITH THE LETTER P!

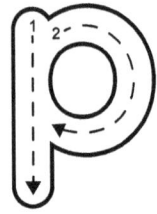

n	P	w	p	v
P	v	i	p	p
A	o	U	P	E
P	c	d	p	y

PERFECT!

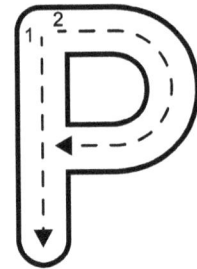
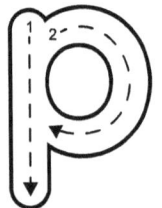

16

KIDDYWINK CREW

POP THE BUBBLES!

POP ALL THE BUBBLES WITH THE LETTER Q!

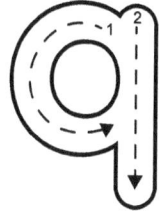

p	Q	j	q	M
f	S	Q	q	O
V	Q	q	O	Q
C	Q	p	g	h

QUITE AMAZING

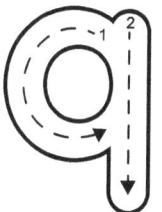

KIDDYWINK CREW

POP THE BUBBLES!

POP ALL THE BUBBLES WITH THE LETTER r!

O	R	b	f	r
r	R	i	Q	f
X	v	R	R	j
r	F	i	X	s

RAD!

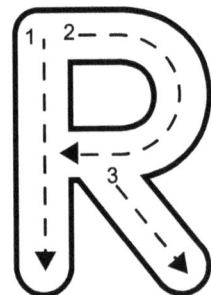

18

KIDDYWINK CREW

POP THE BUBBLES!

POP ALL THE BUBBLES WITH THE LETTER S!

C	S	C	s	p
S	W	S	F	h
S	s	Y	q	B
G	S	I	L	U

SUPER!

KIDDYWINK
CREW

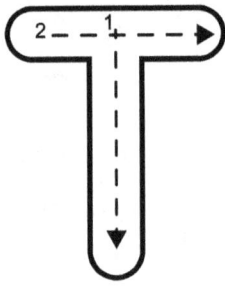

POP THE BUBBLES!

POP ALL THE BUBBLES WITH THE LETTER T!

I	T	E	S	t
F	W	n	B	f
T	t	X	L	T
t	V	J	S	A

TERRIFIC

20

KIDDYWINK CREW

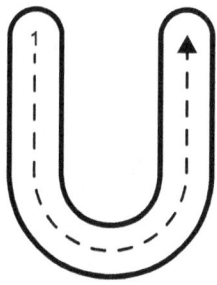

POP THE BUBBLES!

POP ALL THE BUBBLES WITH THE LETTER u!

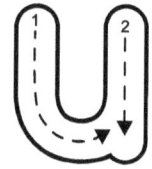

U	v	J	I	C
D	u	s	n	U
j	U	w	u	n
Y	U	u	v	W

UNBEATABLE!

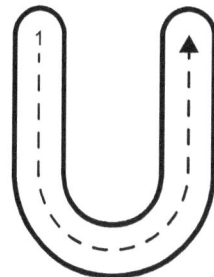

21

KIDDYWINK CREW

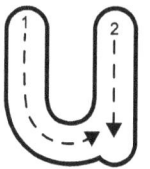

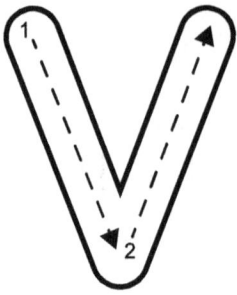

POP THE BUBBLES!

POP ALL THE BUBBLES WITH THE LETTER v!

V	P	J	u	v
F	k	A	v	i
V	W	v	x	l
L	u	V	v	q

VERY IMPRESSIVE!

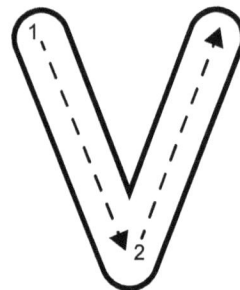

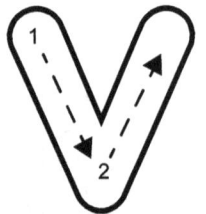

KIDDYWINK CREW

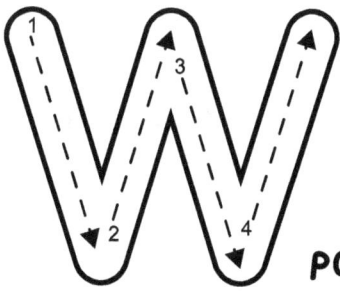

POP THE BUBBLES!
POP ALL THE BUBBLES WITH THE LETTER W!

w	i	q	p	W
k	J	V	W	w
F	j	Q	V	W
w	w	L	O	W

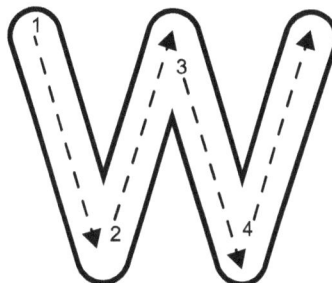

WOW!

KIDDYWINK
CREW

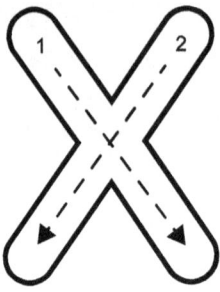

POP THE BUBBLES!
POP ALL THE BUBBLES WITH THE LETTER X!

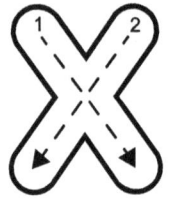

V X T X P

V W X X H

F C U C E

C C G C j

XOXO!

KIDDYWINK
CREW

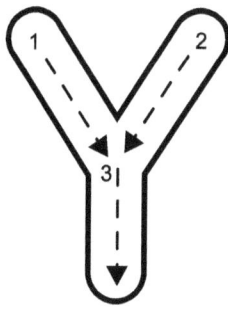

POP THE BUBBLES!

POP ALL THE BUBBLES WITH THE LETTER y!

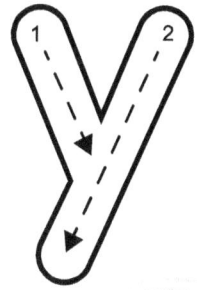

w   Y   n   y   C

P   u   Y   y   v

Y   j   D   c   y

p   y   b   y   Y

YES!

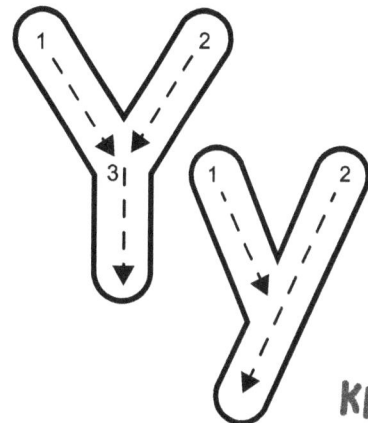

KIDDYWINK
CREW

POP THE BUBBLES!

POP ALL THE BUBBLES WITH THE LETTER z!

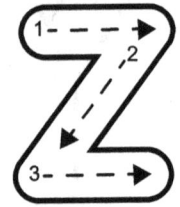

n   z   i   B   z

q   p   f   h   z

N   Z   z   W   z

R   l   L   Z   J

ZESTY

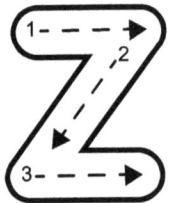

26

KIDDYWINK CREW

Letter Tracing

You did it! Trace each letter one more time!

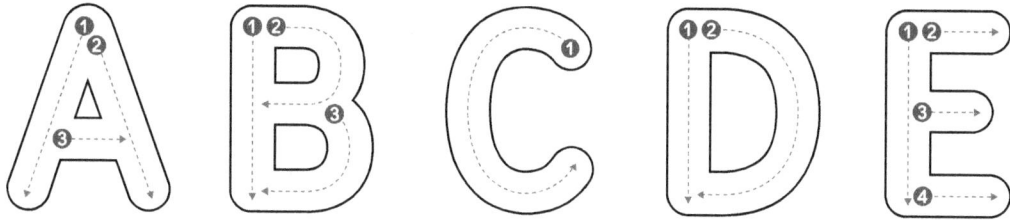

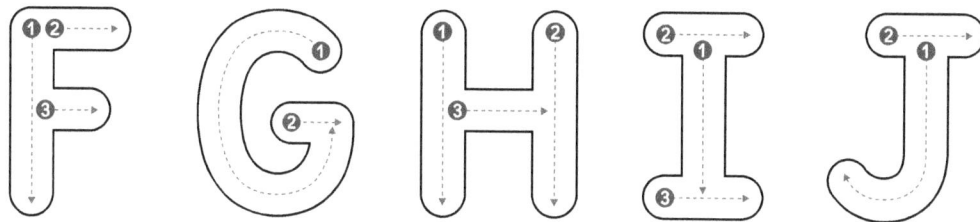

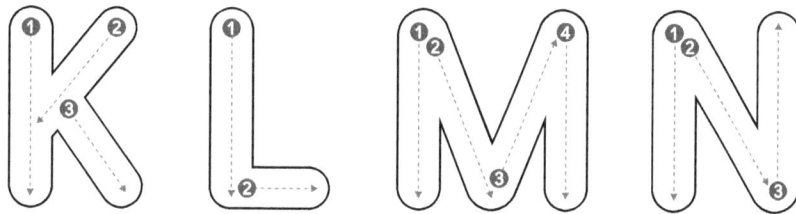

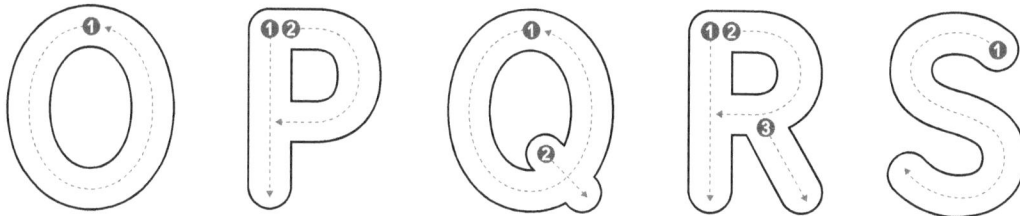

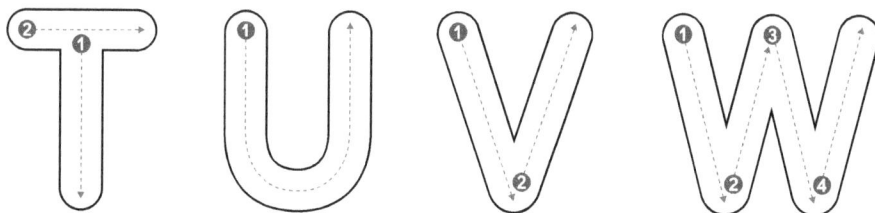

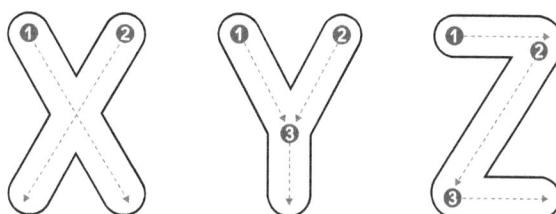

A B C D E

F G H I J

K L M N

O P Q R S

T U V W

X Y Z

POP THE BUBBLES!

POP ALL THE BUBBLES WITH THE NUMBER...

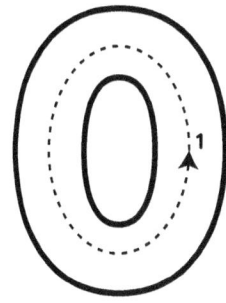

0   1   4   5   2

0   9   2   0   6

0   3   7   7   0

6   0   1   8   0

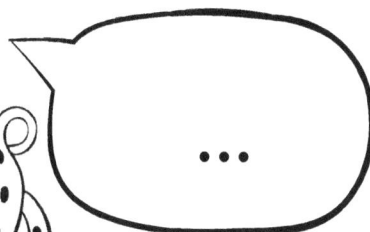

...

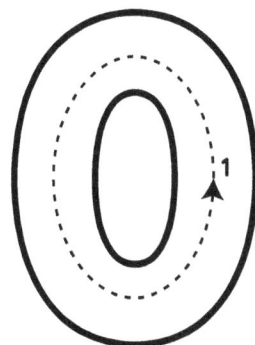

29

POP THE BUBBLES!

POP ALL THE BUBBLES WITH THE NUMBER...

2	1	3	1	6
9	1	0	8	7
1	3	1	7	1
7	0	2	5	1

1!

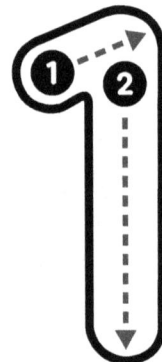

POP THE BUBBLES!

POP ALL THE BUBBLES WITH THE NUMBER...

4	2	2	1	8
6	2	0	2	9
2	7	0	2	1
2	8	2	2	5

1, 2!

POP THE BUBBLES!

POP ALL THE BUBBLES WITH THE NUMBER...

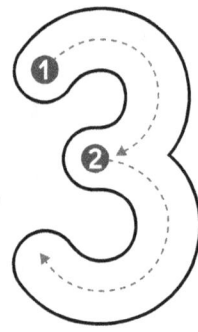

3	2	8	5	8
1	3	3	9	0
3	7	4	3	8
6	3	3	0	6

1, 2, 3!

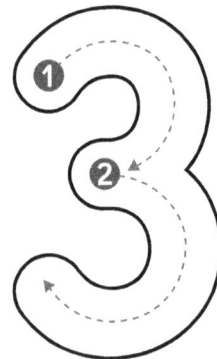

POP THE BUBBLES!

POP ALL THE BUBBLES WITH THE NUMBER...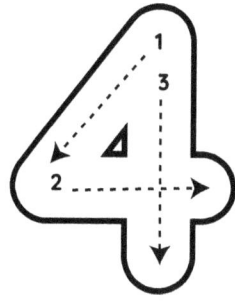

4	8	4	9	1
2	4	3	7	6
4	1	4	3	4
5	4	8	0	4

1, 2, 3, 4!

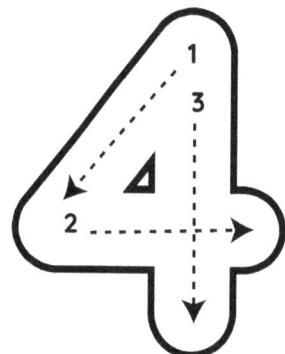

POP THE BUBBLES!

POP ALL THE BUBBLES WITH THE NUMBER...

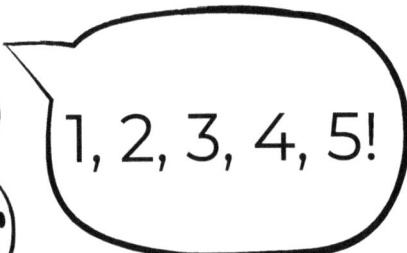

5

4	5	0	2	5
5	8	2	9	5
7	6	5	5	3
0	1	5	5	9

1, 2, 3, 4, 5!

5

POP THE BUBBLES!

POP ALL THE BUBBLES WITH THE NUMBER...

6   7   6   0   1

2   4   6   3   6

6   8   2   6   3

5   6   8   9   6

1, 2, 3, 4, 5, 6!

35

POP THE BUBBLES!

POP ALL THE BUBBLES WITH THE NUMBER...

9	7	1	0	7
2	8	3	7	7
3	6	7	3	7
5	6	7	7	1

1, 2, 3, 4, 5, 6, 7!

POP THE BUBBLES!

POP ALL THE BUBBLES WITH THE NUMBER...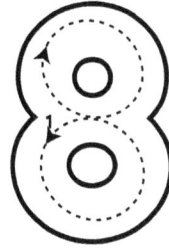

4	8	4	9	1
2	4	3	7	6
4	1	4	3	4
5	4	8	0	4

1, 2, 3, 4, 5, 6, 7, 8!

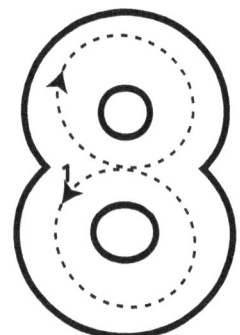

POP THE BUBBLES!

POP ALL THE BUBBLES WITH THE NUMBER...

9	8	1	6	9
9	4	7	9	2
1	0	9	6	9
4	9	3	0	9

1, 2, 3, 4, 5, 6, 7, 8, 9!

POP THE BUBBLES!

POP ALL THE BUBBLES WITH THE NUMBER...

10   11   18   10   0

1   12   10   10   16

13   10   2   13   10

10   10   11   19   20

1, 2, 3, 4, 5, 6, 7, 8, 9, 10!

POP THE BUBBLES!

POP ALL THE BUBBLES WITH THE NUMBER...

11

8   11   12   11   10

3   14   11   19   20

11   11   16   12   13

14   11   15   11   17

1, 2, 3, 4, 5, 6, 7, 8, 9, 10, 11!

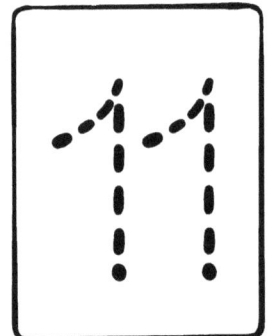

11

POP THE BUBBLES!

POP ALL THE BUBBLES WITH THE NUMBER...

12

10	12	11	12	18
19	17	12	13	12
12	14	17	2	12
12	12	15	16	2

1, 2, 3, 4, 5, 6, 7, 8, 9, 10, 11, 12!

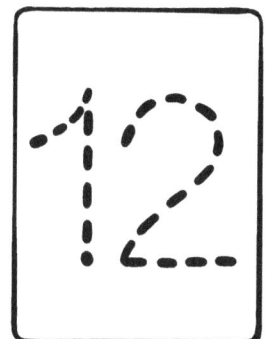

12

41

POP THE BUBBLES!

POP ALL THE BUBBLES WITH THE NUMBER...

13

11	3	19	20	13
16	13	15	13	31
20	13	10	11	13
14	17	13	1	13

1, 2, 3, 4, 5, 6, 7, 8, 9, 10, 11, 12, 13!

13

POP THE BUBBLES!

POP ALL THE BUBBLES WITH THE NUMBER... 14

13   14   10   14   11

20   24   14   4   14

7   17   16   14   14

4   1   14   7   14

1, 2, 3, 4, 5,
6, 7, 8, 9, 10,
11, 12, 13, 14!

14

POP THE BUBBLES!

POP ALL THE BUBBLES WITH THE NUMBER...

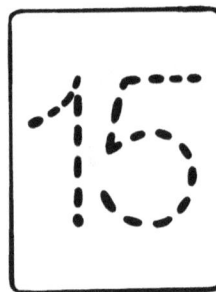

15

5	15	19	20	15
1	15	11	13	18
15	19	15	5	1
15	11	16	17	15

1, 2, 3, 4, 5,
6, 7, 8, 9, 10,
11, 12, 13, 14, 15!

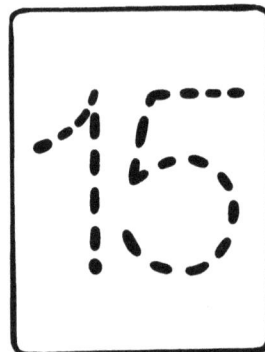

15

POP THE BUBBLES!

POP ALL THE BUBBLES WITH THE NUMBER...

16

16   6   15   16   9

19   20   16   17   18

14   16   16   11   12

16   19   18   12   10

1, 2, 3, 4, 5, 6,
7, 8, 9, 10, 11,
12, 13, 14, 15, 16!

16

POP THE BUBBLES!

POP ALL THE BUBBLES WITH THE NUMBER...

17

19	17	7	11	17
10	17	17	12	15
17	8	17	21	17
71	17	18	20	17

1, 2, 3, 4, 5, 6, 7, 8, 9, 10, 11, 12, 13, 14, 15, 16 17!

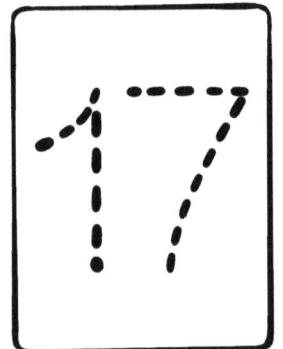

17

POP THE BUBBLES!

POP ALL THE BUBBLES WITH THE NUMBER... 18

18   8   18   19   20

8   18   16   12   18

18   11   10   8   18

16   18   28   18   81

1, 2, 3, 4, 5, 6, 7, 8, 9, 10, 11, 12, 13, 14, 15, 16, 17, 18!

18

POP THE BUBBLES!

POP ALL THE BUBBLES WITH THE NUMBER...

19

19   9   20   19   18

19   9   6   19   12

16   19   10   11   13

19   20   19   10   9

1, 2, 3, 4, 5, 6,
7, 8, 9, 10, 11,
12, 13, 14, 15, 16
17, 18, 19!

19

POP THE BUBBLES!

POP ALL THE BUBBLES WITH THE NUMBER...

20

22   20   19   18   20

26   20   10   13   12

8   20   0   20   10

20   15   5   20   0

1, 2, 3, 4, 5, 6, 7, 8, 9, 10, 11, 12, 13, 14, 15, 16, 17, 18, 19, 20!

20

Number Tracing

You did it! Trace each number one more time!

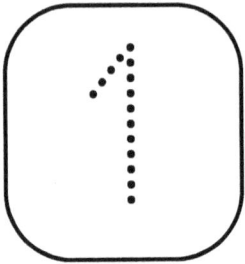

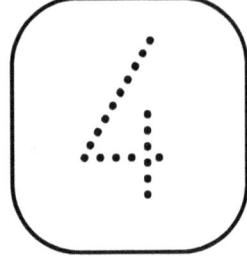

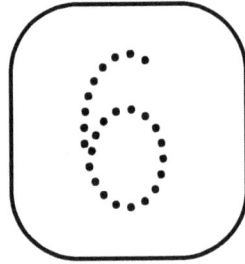

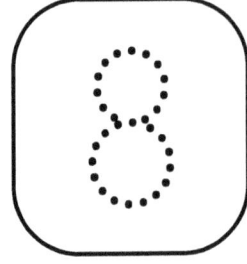

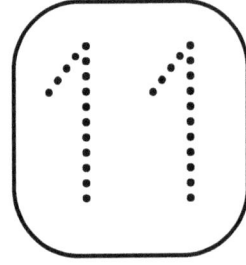

1 2 3 4

5 6 7 8

9 10 11 12

13 14 15 16

17 18 19 20

www.ingramcontent.com/pod-product-compliance
Lightning Source LLC
Chambersburg PA
CBHW081644040426
42449CB00015B/3450